Fantasy Houses

Grayscale Coloring Book

Fairies & Elves Mushroom Homes

Rachel Mintz

Colors Testing Page

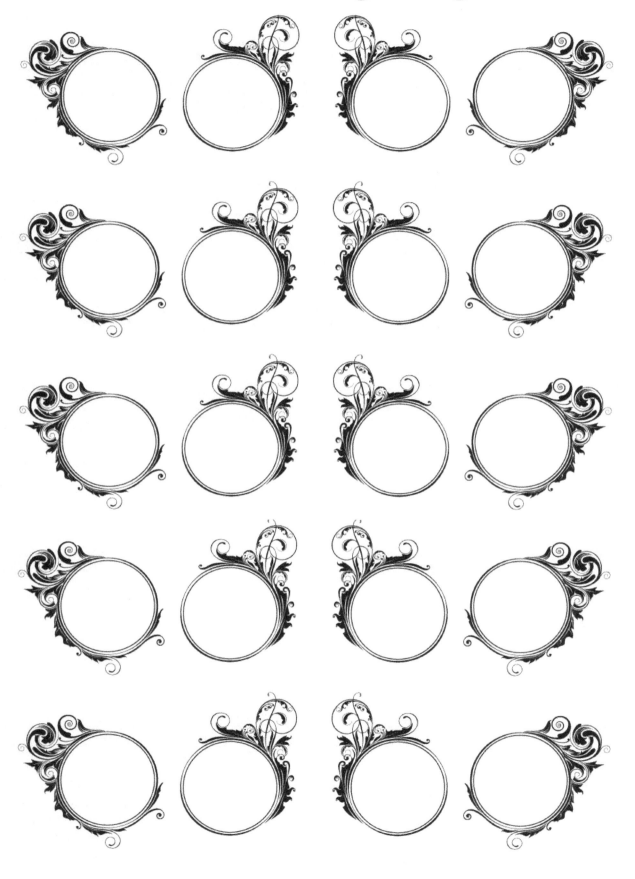

Thank you for coloring with us

Please rate & review this book

Friendship

Vintage Grayscale Art

Rachel Mintz
Coloring Book

In Love

Romantic Grayscale Coloring Book

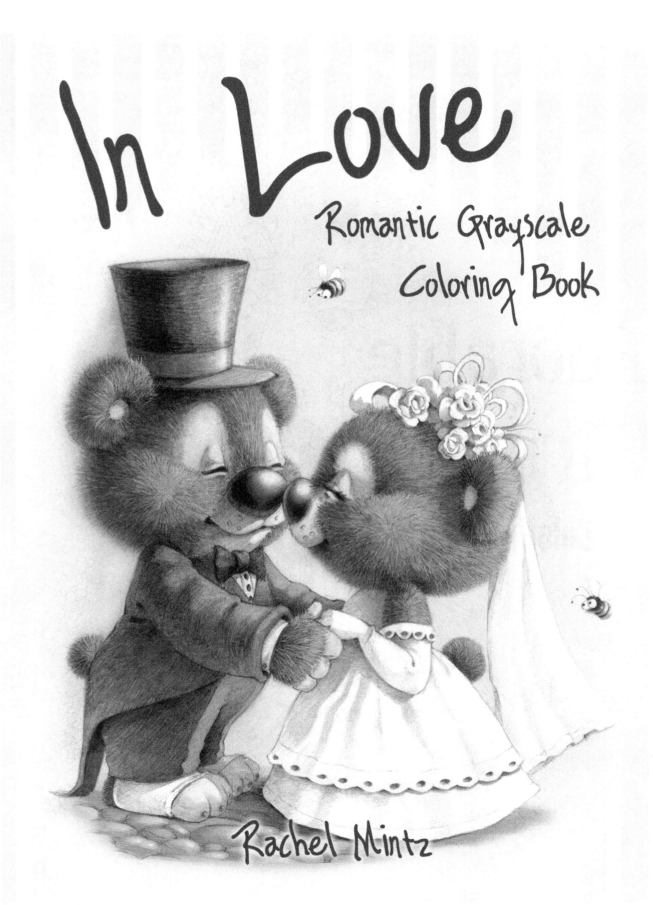

Rachel Mintz

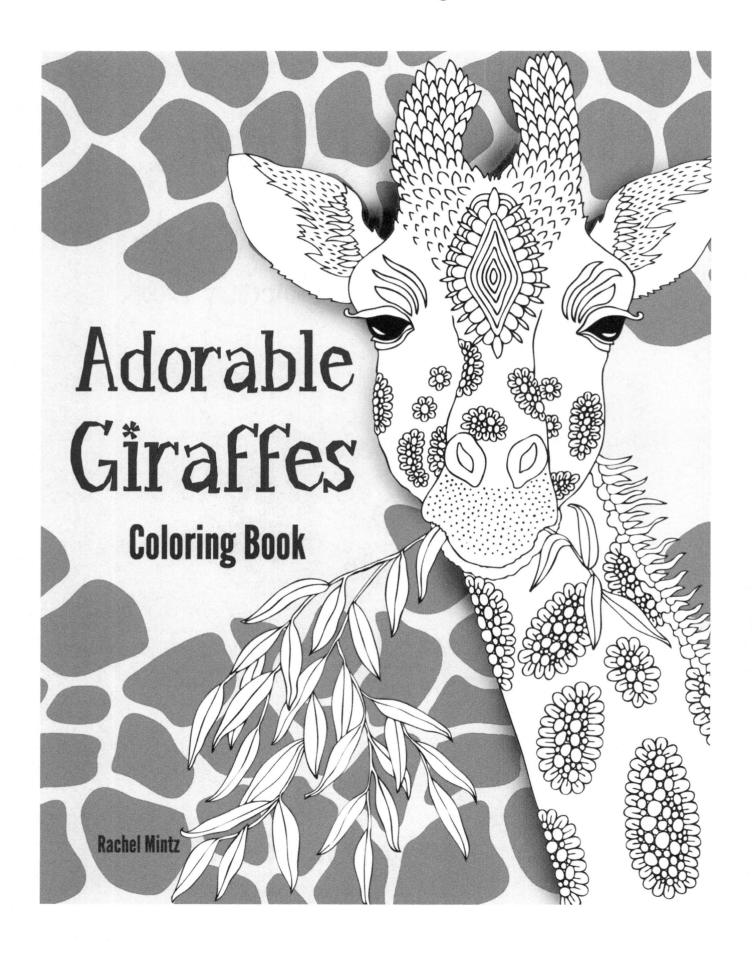

Adorable
Giraffes
Coloring Book

Rachel Mintz

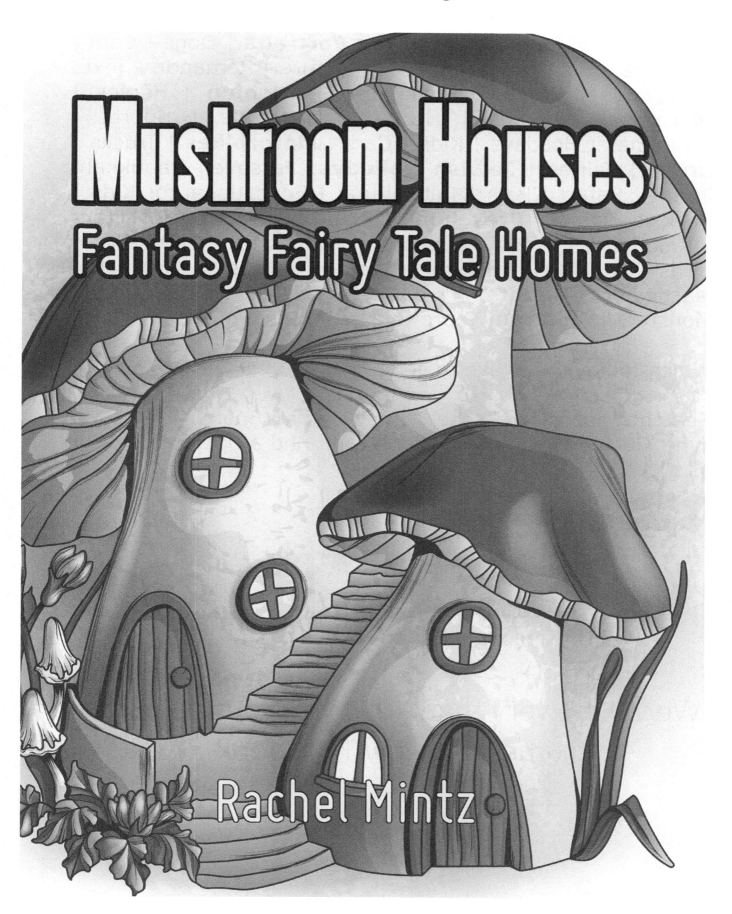

Mushroom Houses
Fantasy Fairy Tale Homes

Rachel Mintz

Look for more RACHEL MINTZ coloring books at Amazon.

Mandalas | Wildlife | Marine Life| **Portraits** | Dogs | Cats | **Flowers** | Skulls | Gothic | Architecture | Romantic | Texts & Sayings | Ethnic | Steampunk | **Fashion** | Horses | Unicorns | Witches | Horror | Grayscale | Sports | Christmas | Holidays | Kids | Cars | **Motorbikes** | Trucks | Urban | Fairies | **Jewish Holidays**: Passover, Hanukkah, Purim | Safari | Pets |Multicultural | Educational for Kids | Back to School | **Preschool & Toddlers** | Army & Military | Knights & Castles | Dragons | Princesses | Butterflies | Birds | Reptiles | Bible | **Stained Glass** | Abstract | Machines | **Robots** | Space & Science | **Zombies** | Monsters | And many more topics..

Which topic do you like to color?

Search Amazon for Rachel Mintz Coloring Books.
Type 'Rachel Mintz + Your Topic' and find a book to color or as a gift.

Thank you for coloring with us

We will be very thankful if you could take the time to review THIS book

Made in the USA
Monee, IL
22 November 2020